STAR WARS®

THE PHANTOM MENACE

Naboo

Far away from the centers of galactic power lies the peaceful planet of Naboo. Its human inhabitants live in harmony and dedicate themselves to the creation of beauty in every area of life. Their capital city, Theed, is one of the most magnificent cities in the galaxy. Beneath the surface of the planet is the fascinating society of the Gungans, an amazingly innovative amphibian race.

Faithful Maiden
The Queen is almost always surrounded by her faithful handmaidens, each of whom would risk her life for her Highness.

Humble Droid
Sitting in the droid hold at the back of the Queen's ship is a humble astromech droid called R2-D2. No one can guess what the future holds for him.

Heroic Captain
The dashing Captain Panaka is one of the Queen's most able and valued soldiers.

Trusty Adviser
Wise Sio Bibble is the Queen's most trusted adviser, a great support when the cares of state weigh heavily on her shoulders.

Agile Sub
The agile Gungan sub is designed to navigate the endless blackness of Naboo's deep waters, but it cannot always avoid their many dangers.

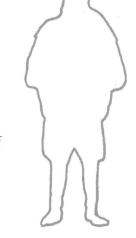

Clumsy Friend
Accident-prone Jar Jar Binks may not be the cleverest of Gungans, but he tries to do what is right and is loyal and caring; a true friend.

Bossy Leader
The tough, bossy leader of the Gungans, Boss Nass seems harsh, but he has a better side to him as well.

Close Friend
The handmaiden Padmé is incredibly close to young Queen Amidala and shares her innermost thoughts.

val Vessel

k, elegant, and fast, the Queen's
l Starship is possibly the
beautiful spaceship in the
xy. It has neither armor
weapons, because it
nes from a land
dicated to peace.

Beast of Burden

These huge beasts of burden
are known as Fambaas. They
have been tamed by the
Gungans and carry their force
shield generators into battle.

Brave Fighter

Although a
planet of
peace,
Naboo still
maintains a small
army. Its soldiers are
brave but few, and
without much
experience of battle.

Royal Robes

The people of Naboo
feel their Queen
should wear the most
splendid clothes and
headdresses. As is
fitting for a queen of
an artistic people,
Amidala dons
exquisite gowns of
striking designs.

Queen of Naboo

The people of Naboo
have chosen to
democratically
elect a king or
queen to rule over
them. Queen
Amidala strives
always to serve her
people, respecting
their laws and the
advice of her
counselors.

Royal Training

Though young, Queen
Amidala is wise beyond
her years and has been
well trained.

Perfect Pilot

Gifted, dedicated,
courageous Ric Olié has
the job that every pilot
dreams of: flying the
Queen's Royal Starship.

Stylish Fighter

Flown by the volunteer Royal
Naboo Security Forces, the Naboo
starfighter is a nimble single-pilot craft,
rimmed with shiny royal chrome.

Animal Transport

Swift and
agile, Kaadus are beloved
by their Gungan masters.
Kaadus have strong senses
of hearing and smell.

Army Transport

Gian Speeders are the main transportation
for the lightly equipped Naboo army. They
resemble civilian speeders, and are just as
much fun to ride!

Dark Forces

Unknown and unsuspected, a strange alliance is about to break the long-standing peace of the Old Republic. Shadowy Darth Sidious has ordered the greedy Trade Federation to move from trade to conquest. Their forces have been working overtime to convert their vast trading fleet into a space navy, with a droid army inside it.

Persistent Traders
They trade across the galaxy, but Neimoidians are so secretive that few outsiders have any idea how their society works.

Tough Tank
The massive armor of this Federation AAT tank protects it from almost all attack, and its powerful armament outguns any opposition.

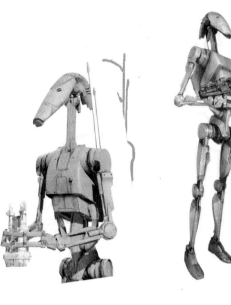

Hard Workers
Like worker ants, every one of the millions of battle droids is controlled from one central computer "brain" in the Trade Federation Droid Control Ship.

Complex Craft
One of the most sophisticated combat craft ever created, the droid starfighter is an actual droid, engineered to operate in deep space.

Droidekas
Most lethal of all the Trade Federation droids, droidekas roll into a ball for swift travel, then uncoil to strike. Well-armed and almost indestructible, even Jedi must beware their power.

Dark Power
As Sith Lord and loyal apprentice of Darth Sidious, the ferocious Darth Maul is a dark shadow of a character, more lethal in battle than all but the most powerful Jedi.

Spy Ship

The ultimate spy ship, this customized Sith Infiltrator is almost undetectable. In its hold it stores sophisticated probe droids, an array of secret weapons, and the amazingly maneuverable Sith speeder bike.

Strange Seat

Nothing illustrates the Neimoidian flair for bizarre design better than the walking chair. Intended to impress, it usually does.

Shadowy Figure

It was thought that the Dark Lords of the Sith had vanished from the galaxy a thousand years ago, but Lord Sidious is using his dark power behind the scenes.

Safe Landing

Descending from orbit like mysterious flying creatures, Trade Federation landing ships carry thousands of battle droids.

Federation Carrier

This monstrous multi troop transport (MTT) ferries Federation battle droids into combat zones of all kinds.

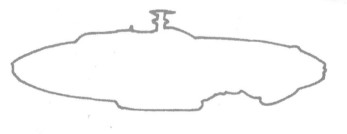

Secret War Freighter

In stealth and in secret, the Trade Federation has converted its fleet of huge cargo ships to carry droids and tanks instead of harmless goods to trade. Concealed weapons are ready to destroy any attempt to escape.

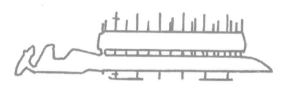

Fast Carrier

Many of the legions of battle droids are transported on speedy troop carriers such as this one.

Single Carrier

The STAP (Single Trooper Aerial Platform) is designed to carry a single battle droid at high speed to terrorize scattered troops and frightened civilians, as the Trade Federation army spreads destruction far and wide.

Extra Vision

These electrobinoculars can detect ultra-violet micro-movement, and heat.

Lethal Weapon

Simple but lethal, the battle droid blaster is carried by every droid in the army.

Tatooine

Wild, lawless, and oppressively hot, the desert planet Tatooine is a magnet for crooks from every corner of the galaxy. Without any government that works, its leading citizen is the infamous crimelord Jabba the Hutt. The one thing that seems to unite the planet's inhabitants is their love for Podracing—the fastest, most dangerous sport there is.

Crime lord
The Hutts are some of the most infamous gangsters in the galaxy, and even among that vile species, Jabba is a legend. Cunning and ruthless, murder, and extortion are his daily business.

Head Protection
Podraces are so fast and so dangerous that no human pilots in them. Until now. Anakin Skywalker has the uncanny ability to challenge the best. This helmet is customized to his own design to optimize vision and hearing.

Special Massage
Native to the planet Ryloth in the Outer Rim, these female Twi'leks are Sebulba the Dug's personal masseuses.

Programmed Killer
A Sith innovation, the probe droid is programmed to find the most elusive targets, using several different scanning and surveillance systems. When a probe droid is after you, there is often no escape.

Droid Service
They look comic but are actually essential. Pit droids help maintain and service the Podracers, a truly tricky task.

Speedy Racer
Anakin built this Podracer himself in his own workshop, from scrap. With numerous clever modifications, it could well be the fastest racer ever.

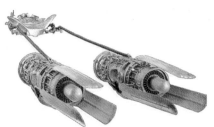

Surprise Speeder
Although it has no weapons, shields, or sensors, the Sith speeder is a sight to fear as it is astonishingly fast and usually piloted by the dreaded Darth Maul.

Champion Racer
The reigning Podrace champion, Sebulba has set his heart (what there is of it) on winning the great Boonta Classic race—by fair means or foul.

True Mother
Enslaved by Watto on Tatooine, Shmi Skywalker asks very little for herself. Her hopes are focused entirely on her son, Anakin. Aware of his special gifts, she hopes he will one day be free.

Bizarre Beast
Bizarre beasts of burden, eopies are used all over Tatooine. Few take the trouble to treat them well.

Young Force
Gifted and popular, Anakin Skywalker is intelligent and mature beyond his years. Attuned to the Force, Anakin is the only human on Tatooine who can race Podracers. But the boy dreams of one day becoming a space pilot, or even a Jedi Knight.

View Point
There are dozens of 3-D cameras around the Mos Espa Podrace course, feeding pictures into screens for excited fans to watch.

Anakin's Droid
This seemingly amateurish droid is one of Anakin's major projects. He has been building it for nearly a year, and his ingenious programming gives C-3PO capacities that no one could suspect.

Green hunters
The green-skinned Rodians come from the planet Rodia. They are natural fighters, and many become bounty hunters.

Typical Podracer
This Podracer, like all others, is custom-built around two mighty engines and a tiny cockpit.

Powerful Podracer
One of the most powerful Podracers ever invented, Sebulba's machine is also equipped with dirty tricks to sabotage rivals.

Tough Customer
Harsh, clever, and very, very sharp in business dealings, Watto runs a junk shop in Mos Espa on Tatooine, assisted by his slaves Anakin and Shmi Skywalker.

Coruscant

Ancient capital of the Republic, the fabled city-planet is a byword for splendor and wealth. But something is rotten at the heart of this planet on which so many worlds depend.

Respected Jedi
Unconventional and a loner, Qui-Gon Jinn is none the less a highly respected and powerful Jedi Master.

Troubled Leader
Head of the government, Chancellor Valorum strives for good, yet is endlessly hampered by unfounded accusations and baseless scandals.

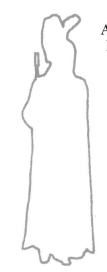

Armed Guard
Do not be deceived by the ceremonial uniform. The Senate guards are elite troops, and lethal whether armed or not.

Talented Pupil
Cautious and responsible, Obi-Wan Kenobi is a very talented Jedi Padawan. He is fiercely devoted to his Master, Qui-Gon, and together they make a good team.

Bad Senator
Working in the corrupt Senate has made Tonbuck Toora greedy and lazy. Many of her best friends are criminals, liars, and cheats.

Wise Master
The aged Jedi Master, Yoda, is very wise and respected Over the year he has trained many Jedi, and they look to him for guidance.

Senior Jedi
A Senior Jedi on the Council, Mace Windu is wise in the ways of the Force, but mistakenly believes that the Sith are extinct.

Red Cruiser
Assembled in the great Corellian shipyards, the red Republic Cruiser carries Jedi Knights, diplomats, and ambassadors around the galaxy.

Power Seeker
Senator Palpatine comes from Naboo. He seems well-meaning and idealistic, but secretly yearns for power.

SPACECRAFT, VEHICLES, DROIDS, AND EQUIPMENT

Gian Speeder

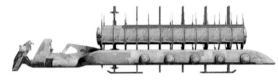

Federation Troop Carrier

Battle Droid
Blaster

Electrobinoculars

Battle
Droid

Naboo Starfighter

Queen's Royal
Starship

Anakin's
Helmet

R2-D2

Podrace
Viewscreen

Battle Droid
Commander

Droideka

Sith Infiltrator

Neimoidian
Mechno-chair

Federation
AAT

SPACECRAFT, VEHICLES, DROIDS, AND EQUIPMENT

Gian Speeder

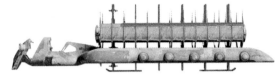

Federation Troop Carrier

Battle Droid
Blaster

Electrobinoculars

Battle
Droid

Naboo Starfighter

Queen's Royal
Starship

Anakin's
Helmet

R2-D2

Battle Droid
Commander

Podrace
Viewscreen

Droideka

Sith Infiltrator

Neim
Mechno-cha

Federation
AAT

HEROES AND VILLAINS

Darth
Maul

Queen
Amidala

Senator
Palpatine

Senate
Guard

Qui-Gon
Jinn

Jar Jar
Binks

Rodian

Senator Tonbuck Toora

Ric Olié

Twi'lek

Kaadu

Yoda

Queen
Amidala

Boss
Nass

Neimoidian

Captain Panaka

HEROES AND VILLAINS

Darth
Maul

Queen
Amidala

Senator
Palpatine

Senate
Guard

Qui-Gon
Jinn

Jar Jar
Binks

Rodian

Senator Tonbuck Toora

Ric Olié

Twi'lek

Kaadu

Yoda

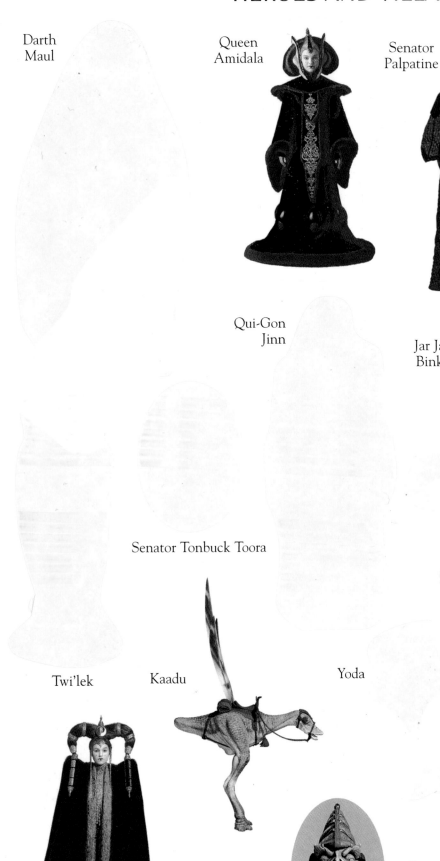

Queen
Amidala

Boss
Nass

Neimoidian

Captain Panaka

HEROES AND VILLAINS

Sio
Bibble

Padmé

Anakin
Skywalker

Queen's Handmaiden

Neimoidian

Sebulba

Naboo
soldier

Darth
Sidious

Chancellor
Valorum

Obi-Wan
Kenobi

Mace
Windu

Shmi Skywalker

Watto

Queen
Amidala

Fambaa

Jabba the
Hutt

Eopie

HEROES AND VILLAINS

Sio Bibble

Neimoidian

Padmé

Anakin Skywalker

Queen's Handmaiden

Sebulba

Naboo Soldier

Obi-Wan Kenobi

Mace Windu

Chancellor Valorum

Darth Sidious

Shmi Skywalker

Watto

Fambaa

Queen Amidala

Jabba the Hutt

Eopie

SPACECRAFT, VEHICLES, DROIDS, AND EQUIPMENT

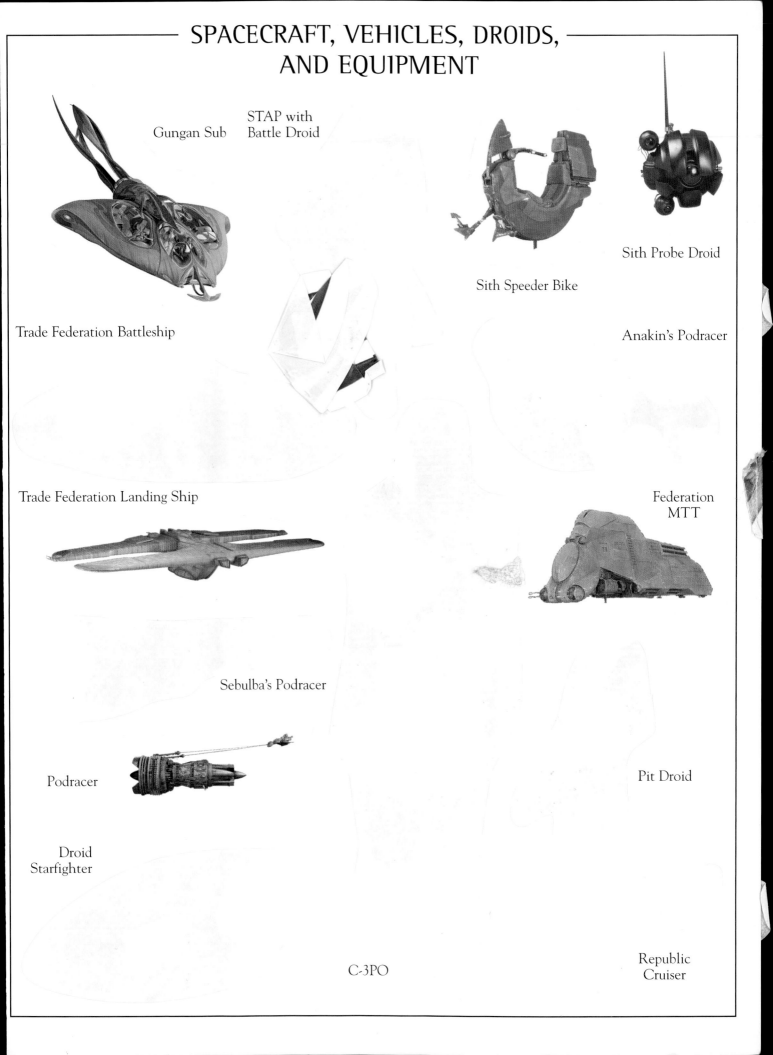

Gungan Sub

STAP with Battle Droid

Sith Probe Droid

Sith Speeder Bike

Trade Federation Battleship

Anakin's Podracer

Trade Federation Landing Ship

Federation MTT

Sebulba's Podracer

Podracer

Pit Droid

Droid Starfighter

C-3PO

Republic Cruiser

SPACECRAFT, VEHICLES, DROIDS, AND EQUIPMENT

Gungan Sub

STAP with Battle Droid

Sith Probe Droid

Sith Speeder Bike

Trade Federation Battleship

Anakin's Podracer

Trade Federation Landing Ship

Federation MTT

Sebulba's Podracer

Podracer

Pit Droid

Droid Starfighter

C-3PO

Republic Cruiser

ATTACK OF THE CLONES

Allies of the Republic

The stability of the Republic is uncertain, but the peacekeeping force of Jedi defends the Republic's authority wherever it is threatened as representatives from across the galaxy argue endlessly in the Senate.

Naboo Senator
As the Queen of Naboo Padmé Amidala won the lasting devotion of her people. Now as the elected Senator, Padmé represents her homeworld in the Senate.

The One?
Anakin Skywalker has learned the ways of the Force under the guidance of Obi-Wan Kenobi, but he is impatient with the rules and often thinks that he knows best. Many Jedi believe he is the prophesized Chosen One who will bring balance to the Force.

Jedi Weapon
All Jedi build their own lightsabers when they are Padawan learners. Obi-Wan Kenobi's lightsaber has a blue blade and a spherical end.

Padawan Weapon
Jedi Padawans often build their lightsabers to look like their Master's, as a symbol of respect.

Jedi Teacher
Obi-Wan Kenobi is a dedicated Jedi Knight, and tries hard to teach Anakin Skywalker the ways of the Force. Having witnessed the death of his Master, he knows the strength of the Sith from first-hand experience.

War Hero
After his part in the Battle of Naboo, the inhabitants of his home world made Jar Jar Associate Planetary Representative in the Galactic Senate.

Jedi Team
Luminara is a Jedi with amazing lightsaber abilities. She can bend her body into impossible moves during combat. Her Padawan learner, Barriss, uses the Force in order to fight in tandem with her partner.

Jedi Master
Yoda is about 900 years old but his skill in using the Force gives him amazing strength and speed. Yoda rarely uses his lightsaber, but when he does, his abilities overwhelm his opponents.

Politcal Aide
Sly Moore is Palapatine's aide. She has lots of power as she controls who sees the Supreme Chancellor. Moore is an Umbaran, a species known for its abilities to influence and control others.

Supreme Chancellor
Palpatine took office when the previous Supreme Chancellor seemed unable to rule effectively. Always declaring that his new laws are in the best interests of the Republic, they also seem to increase his own personal power.

Alderaan Senator
Bail Organa is the Senator for his home planet Alderaan. Most Senators are corrupt and accept money in return for their vote. Bail Organa is one of the few Senators who refuses take part in the political corruption.

Head of Security
Captain Typho is the head of Senator Amidala's security. He is the nephew of Captain Panaka, who served Padmé while she was Queen of Naboo.

Senator in Combat
As a Queen and a Senator, Padmé has only had limited weapons training. However, she has natural skill with a blaster in combat.

Jedi Warrior
Mace Windu is one of the best living lightsaber masters in the Jedi order. His lightsaber has a purple blade.

Secret Guard
Palpatine has kept the details of the Red Guard's training secret. No one knows where the guards come from. Their weapons are lethal force pikes.

Togrutan Jedi
Shaak Ti is a Togruta, a species that lives in tribes on the planet Shili. She can fight well in group combat because she is used to moving in dense crowds on her home planet.

Speaker of the Senate
Mas Amedda is the Speaker of the Senate and has to keep order during debates. A Chagrian from Champala, he is fiercely loyal to Palpatine.

Threats to the Republic

The Separatist confederacy includes many commercial businesses, whose only concern is profit. Their leader is Count Dooku, an ex-Jedi. Bounty hunters are hired by the Separatists to kill key Senators in order to cause unrest.

Separatist Leader
Count Dooku was once a brilliant Jedi Master. He left the Jedi order after the Battle of Naboo, disillusioned with the Republic and what it had become. He openly contests the Republic's authority.

From Jedi to Sith
Dooku reveals his true nature when he uses Sith lightning. It is difficult to deflect and causes terrible pain and weakness to the victim.

Untrustworthy Neimoidians
Nute Gunray is the viceroy of the Trade Federation. He ordered the blockade and invasion of Naboo. His assistant, Rune Haako, a fellow Neimoidian, is as conniving as Gunray is.

Unusual Lightsaber
As a Jedi Master, Dooku abandoned the lightsaber he built as a Padawan (as Jedi sometimes do) and created a highly individual design, like no other in existence at that time.

Eight-Legged Droid
The Commerce Guild's dwarf spider droids are built with striding legs to walk across difficult terrain. They hunt down individuals attempting to avoid tribute payments, and were also used in the Clone Wars.

Missile Launcher
The Hailfire droids of the InterGalactic Banking Clan search out those who might not pay back their loans. Their missile launchers fire "late payment notices."

Laser-Armed Droid
Built by the Commerce Guild, the homing spider droid is the most feared weapon of the Separatists' Armed Forces. Equipped with a homing laser that fires at light speed, it is almost impossible to defend against.

Geonosian Leader

Archduke Poggle the Lesser is the ruler of all the underground hives on Geonosis. The insectoid Geonosians have increased their riches through the production of battle droids for the Separatist armies.

Upgraded Battle Droid

The super battle droid is an upgraded model of the standard battle droid. They have reinforced joints and tougher armor than their predecessors, but use the same internal parts. They are supplied to the Separatist armies by the wealthy Trade Federation.

Insectoid Army

On Geonosis, drones serve the aristocracy. Soldier drones are grown especially to fight in the Geonosian arena, and in battle. They grow quickly, and are ready to fight after just six years.

Geonosian Weapon

Geonosian soldier drones use sonic blasters as their weapon of choice. It produces a destructive sonic ball, which only discharges once it has reached its target.

Trained to Kill

Zam Wesell is a bounty hunter and contract killer, and is paid well to carry out assassinations. She is able to change her appearance, in order to resemble many different humanoid lifeforms.

Poisoned Dart

This saberdart silences Zam just as she is about to reveal who she is working for. It serves as a clue, however, leading Obi-Wan Kenobi to Jango Fett.

Assassin's Pistol

Zam's trusty KYD-21 blaster pistol is always by her side. It is small enough to hide when she is shape-shifting into an inconspicuous lifeform.

Sniper Rifle

Zam carries a projectile rifle at her employer's insistence. She uses it in the dark when she wants to remain invisible.

Defensive Battle Droids

These assault robots are manufactured by the Trade Federation for the Separatist armies. They have their own defensive shields and can withstand attack from standard blaster weapons and lightsabers.

Speedy Getaway

To prevent being traced, Zam usually steals vehicles when she is working on a job. However, if she needs a reliable and speedy vehicle she uses her own airspeeder for transport.

Galactic Inhabitants

The galaxy is home to many strange species. Four-armed chefs serve food to Jedi, mysterious Sand People roam the deserts of Tatooine, and vicious beasts are enslaved and made to fight in Geonosian arenas.

Four-Armed Chef

Dexter Jettster from Besalisk, owns and runs "Dexter's Diner," a simple café in Coruscant's industrial Coco Town. When Obi-Wan Kenobi pays him a visit, Dex's keen powers of observation and good memory are very helpful to the Jedi.

Arena Beast

Used as an arena beast on the planet of Geonosis, the nexu is a fearsome creature. Its second pair of eyes sees in infrared, enabling it to pick up heat signatures of warm-blooded life-forms. The nexu seizes its prey in its mouth and then shakes the victim to death.

Shady Character

Slythmongers hang around nightclubs, selling the latest fashionable narcotics (such as Death Sticks) to the club patrons. Death Sticks are powerful drugs, which shorten the user's lifespan the more you take them.

Loyal Droid

Padmé's faithful astromech droid has earned her affection through years of loyal service. Throughout the galaxy, droids are often looked down upon but R2-D2 is a remarkable robot with a spirited personality.

Tatooine Family

Owen Lars is Shmi Skywalker's step-son and Anakin's step-brother. He now lives with his father, Cliegg, and girlfriend, Beru, on Tatooine as Shmi was captured by Tusken Raiders. The young Anakin Skywalker built C-3PO out of scrounged parts and left the droid with his mother when he departed to be trained as a Jedi.

Farm Settler

Cliegg Lars came to Tatooine to start a new life as a moisture farmer. He met slave Shmi Skywalker and fell in love with her. However, before they could marry, he had to buy her from Watto, the junk dealer, in order to free her.

Tribal Child

Tusken Raider children are called Uli-ah. They wear unisex clothes that protect them from the sun, wind, and sand. Like their elders, they wear garments that hide all flesh. Tusken children are fully accepted into the tribe when they reach 15 years of age and pass difficult trials.

Cloning Experts

Kaminoans are a very tall species who are experts in cloning technology. When their planet was flooded, they had to adapt. Their cities are built on stilts and they rely on imports from other worlds to maintain their society.

Deadly Claws

Acklays come from the planet Vendaxa. They are terrifying arena beasts, as their huge sharp claws can pierce and kill their prey with a single blow.

Tusken Raider Weapon

The traditional weapon of the Sand People is the gaderffii or "gaffi" stick. They are made from krayt dragon horn and salvaged plating from spacecraft wrecks found in the Tatooine desert.

Mysterious Desert-Dwellers

Tusken Raiders, also called Sand People, are native to Tatooine. They live in tribal clans and blend seamlessly into the desert landscape. They take care to cover up all their flesh, and are fiercely defensive of their precious water supply.

Kaminoan Transport

Aiwhas are creatures that can fly and swim with equal ease. They fill their body tissue with water when they want to swim and wring it out when they want to fly. They are used by Kaminoans for transportation.

Vicious Plant-Eaters

Reeks are herbivores, but if starved long enough will turn carnivorous. They come from the Codian Moon, but are captured to perform as arena beasts for the Geonosians. They will eventually die if fed on meat alone, so they are given just enough plant food to survive.

Preparing for War

With tension rising between the Republic and the Separatists, conflict becomes inevitable. Each side builds up its armies and weapons of destruction in the race to become ready for war.

Ready for Battle
Clone trooper body armor is lightweight and heavy duty. It is made up of 20 plates and is based on Mandalorian armor.

Trooper Blaster
The DC-15 rifle is one of two blaster weapons issued to clone troopers. Both weapons shoot plasma bolts using a small amount of Tibanna gas.

Patrol Ship
Jango Fett's ship, *Slave I*, was built for the purpose of patrolling the prison moon of Oovo 4, in order to prevent escapes.

Air Fighter/Transporter
Republic gunships are designed to attack the battle droid army of the Separatists from the air. Each ship is heavily armed and also provides infantry transport.

Growing Army
A mysterious Jedi Sifo-Dyas ordered the Kaminoans to create a vast army using DNA from Jango Fett. The clones grow at twice the rate of normal humans.

Contract Killer
Jango Fett is a ruthlessly efficient bounty hunter. After the murder of his parents, he was raised by the Mandalorian army. The Jedi destroyed this army, but Jango Fett still wears the armored uniform

Flying Power
Jango Fett has two jetpacks. This one is more heavily armored.

Six-Legged Transport Vehicle
Clone trooper transport vehicles and combat machines have been made to assist the clones. This All-Terrain Tactical Enforcer (AT-TE) has six articulated legs

Warship
Republic assault ships transport the gunships that carry the clone troopers into battle against the Separatist army.

Jango's Clone Son
Boba Fett is an exact clone of his father. Jango Fett requested that the Kaminoans provide him with a "son" as payment for his services as the model for the clone trooper army.

HEROES AND VILLAINS

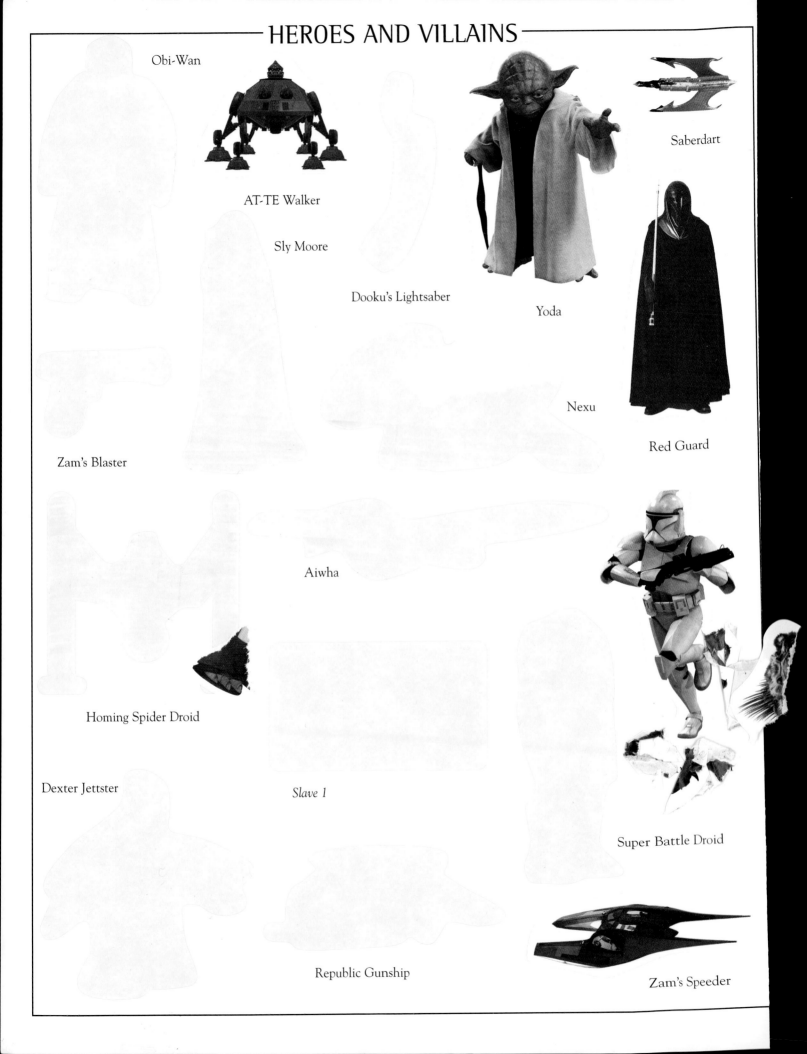

Obi-Wan

AT-TE Walker

Sly Moore

Dooku's Lightsaber

Yoda

Saberdart

Nexu

Red Guard

Zam's Blaster

Aiwha

Homing Spider Droid

Dexter Jettster

Slave 1

Super Battle Droid

Republic Gunship

Zam's Speeder

HEROES AND VILLAINS

Obi-Wan

Saberdart

AT-TE Walker

Sly Moore

Dooku's Lightsaber

Yoda

Nexu

Red Guard

Zam's Blaster

Aiwha

Homing Spider Droid

Dexter Jettster

Slave 1

Clone Trooper

Super Battle Droid

Republic Gunship

Zam's Speeder

HEROES AND VILLAINS

Jango Fett

Owen, Beru,
and C-3PO

Anakin

Hailfire
Droid

Padmé

Reek

Shaak Ti

Clone Trooper Rifle

Droideka

Obi-Wan's
Lightsaber

Republic
Assault Ship

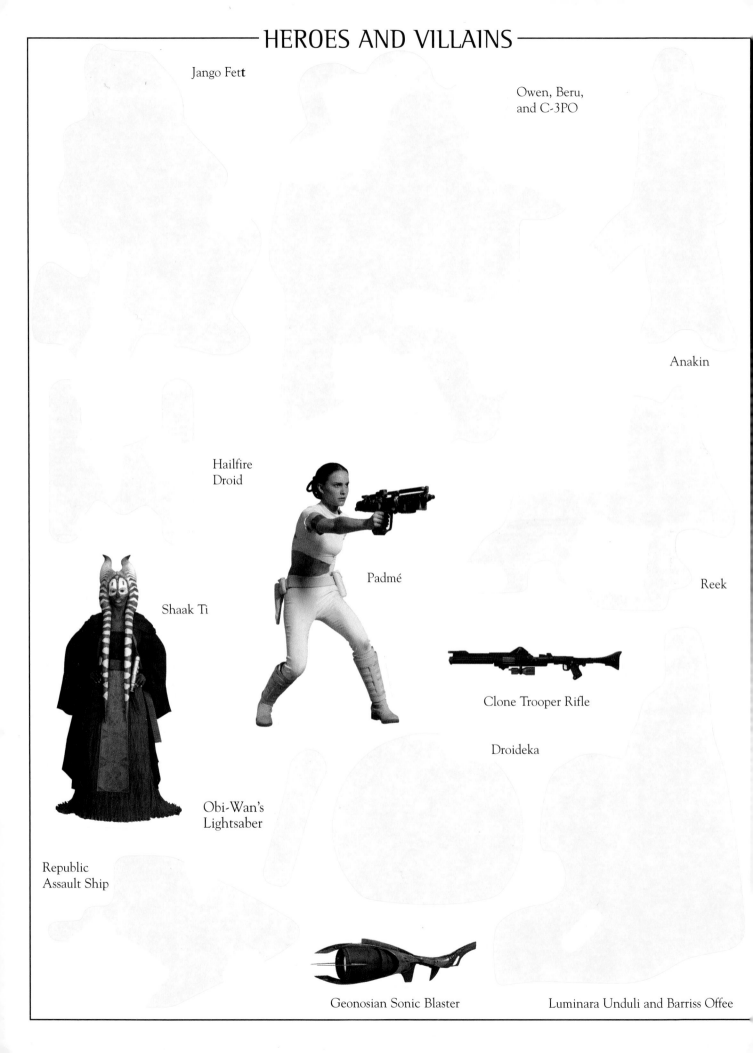

Geonosian Sonic Blaster

Luminara Unduli and Barriss Offee

HEROES AND VILLAINS

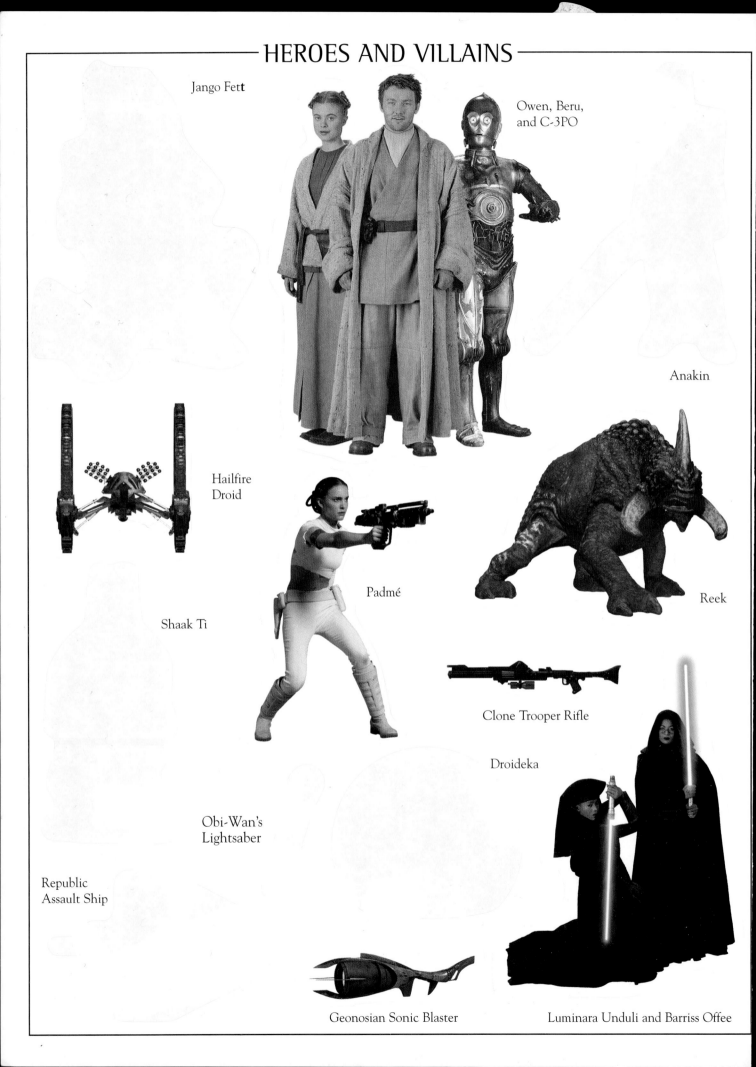

Jango Fett

Owen, Beru, and C-3PO

Anakin

Hailfire Droid

Shaak Ti

Padmé

Reek

Clone Trooper Rifle

Droideka

Obi-Wan's Lightsaber

Republic Assault Ship

Geonosian Sonic Blaster

Luminara Unduli and Barriss Offee

HEROES AND VILLAINS

R2-D2

Clone Youth

Gaderffii

Jar Jar

Poggle the Lesser

Zam Wesell

Jango Fett's Jetpack

Zam's Rifle

Acklay

Uli-ah

Dwarf Spider Droid

Typho

Rune Haako and Nute
Gunray

Palpatine

Geonosian
Soldier Drone

HEROES AND VILLAINS

R2-D2

Clone Youth

Gaderffii

Jar Jar

Zam Wesell

Poggle the Lesser

Jango Fett's Jetpack

Zam's Rifle

Acklay

Uli-ah

Dwarf Spider Droid

Typho

Rune Haako and Nute
Gunray

Palpatine

Geonosian
Soldier Drone

Tusken Raiders

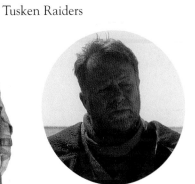

Cliegg Lars

Sith Lightning

Mace Windu

Bail Organa

Anakin's
Lightsaber

Count Dooku

Kaminoans

Mas Amedda

Senator
Amidala

Young Boba

Slythmonger

Tusken Raiders

Cliegg Lars

Sith Lightning

Mace Windu

Anakin's
Lightsaber

Bail Organa

Count Dooku

Mas Amedda

Kaminoans

Young Boba

Senator
Amidala

Slythmonger

REVENGE OF THE SITH

Loyalist Defenders

After 1,000 years of peace, the terrible Clone Wars have begun. Armies of droid soldiers are on the march. Leading the Republic's counter-attack are the Jedi Knights and their clone army, supported by Supreme Chancellor Palpatine.

Teacher and Friend
Obi-Wan Kenobi is a calm, courageous Jedi Master. He is also Anakin's teacher and friend. Yet the Clone Wars will test their friendship to its limits—and beyond!

Troublesome Jedi
Anakin Skywalker has come a long way from his childhood on Tatooine. Now he is famed for his skill and daring as a Jedi Knight. But his destiny does not lie on the light side of the Force.

Double Life
Padmé Amidala is the Senator for her home planet of Naboo. But, secretly, she is also Anakin Skywalker's wife. They must keep their love hidden because a Jedi is forbidden to marry.

Trusty Ship
Anakin flies into action in his small, fast Jedi Interceptor. He and Obi-Wan Kenobi have flown side-by-side on many missions together since the outbreak of war.

Wise Master
The wisest of all the Jedi is Yoda. But even he is troubled by the scale of the war that has broken out in the galaxy. He is determined to track down the Sith Lord who is masterminding the troubles.

Two Droids
When Anakin Skywalker was a boy, he built a droid, whom he named C-3PO. This loyal but timid droid is now assigned to help Anakin's wife, Padmé. R2-D2 was once Padmé's droid, but now he assists Anakin in his Interceptor.

Jedi in the Field
Jedi Master Ki-Adi-Mundi is sent to fight on Mygeeto. Also known as the "Crystal World," this planet is controlled by the aggressive InterGalactic Banking Clan, which is helping to fund the conflict.

Teamwork

Obi-Wan Kenobi flies a red Jedi Interceptor into battle. All Jedi pilots are assisted by an astromech droid, which is plugged into one of the wing supports.

Senator and Rebel

Bail Organa is Senator for the planet Alderaan. He believes that Supreme Chancellor Palpatine has become dangerously powerful. He wants to form a group of rebel Senators to stand up to him.

Jedi Temple Defender

Shaak Ti is an alien Jedi Knight. While most of her fellow Jedi are at war across the galaxy, Shaak Ti remains on Coruscant to oversee the defence of the Jedi Temple—a highly dangerous task.

Bold Master

Mace Windu is a disciplined leader of the Jedi Knights. He is one of the first Jedi to realise that Supreme Chancellor Palpatine is really an evil Sith Lord in disguise. He leads a group of Jedi to confront Palpatine—with dire consequences.

Skilled Pilot

Anakin Skywalker is one of the best pilots that has ever lived. When he is at the controls of a spaceship, he is daring and fearless. He puts trust in his incredible ability to use the power of the Force.

Jedi in Crisis

Kit Fisto is hand-picked by Mace Windu to confront Supreme Chancellor Palpatine. Windu knows Fisto is a versatile fighter, but he will face his ultimate challenge when he goes against this Sith Lord!

Brave and Loyal

Agen Kolar is a species called a Zabrak from the planet Iridonia. He agrees to support Mace Windu in his dangerous confrontation with Palpatine.

Plo Koon's Starfighter

Jedi Master Plo Koon sits on the Jedi High Council, the body that oversees the Jedi's activities. He uses a distinctive Jedi starfighter specially equipped for missions throughout the galaxy.

Clone Army

The origins of the clone army are still a mystery. The army was built and trained on a remote planet, but the Republic only heard of it just before war broke out. Now the clones report directly to Palpatine—but can he be trusted?

Mighty Battleship
The *Venator*-class Star Destroyer can blast enemy ships into pieces with its heavy turbolaser guns, which are positioned around the sides.

Armed Troops
Clone troopers are armed with massive DC-15 rifles, which fire plasma bolts. Soldiers sometimes carry smaller DC-15 blasters, for close-range combat.

Flight Specialist
Clone pilots are trained to fly many different types of spaceship, from small V-wing fighters to gigantic Star Destroyers. Their high-visibility helmets allow clear sightlines through the cockpit screens.

Small Walker
The AT-RT (All Terrain Recon Transport) walks on two legs and carries a single clone trooper in its open cockpit. Its blaster cannon can destroy small targets.

... ...dier
The first clone ...diers were identical ...ies of a bounty ...nter named Jango ...t. They were born and ...sed on the remote planet Kamino. From an early age, each clone was trained in the arts of war.

Clone Trooper
Clone soldiers are specialists in many types of battlefield. Different regiments of clone troopers are identified by the colored stripes on their white armor.

Swamp Speeder
These fast, highly armed speeders zip over land or water, marking out their terrain with deadly precision. They are particularly useful on swampy planets such as the Wookiee homeworld, Kashyyyk.

Rugged Fighter

Tough, powerful ARC-170 fighters feature two massive cannons, one on each wing. They can blast much larger opponents out of the skies. The wings split when in attack position.

Reliable Officer?

Commander Bly is assigned to liberate the planet Felucia from Separatist control. The Jedi who work with Bly trust him for his keen understanding of enemy tactics, so they are totally unprepared for his sinister change of battle plan.

Battle Strike

Swarms of small V-wing fighters fly into battle, each one piloted by clones. They provide back-up to the Jedi in their own fighters, and can deliver a relentless stream of deadly laser fire.

Clone Trooper

In the Clone Wars, troopers fight on planets all around the galaxy. Because each planet is very different, they are trained to adapt to strange new terrain.

Rescue Mission

ARC-170 fighters provide fire cover for Anakin and Obi-Wan in their Jedi Interceptors. The Jedi are trying to rescue Supreme Chancellor Palpatine, who is being held prisoner aboard this massive Separatist ship.

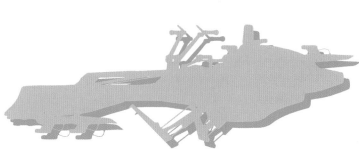

Speeder Bike

Clone troopers ride these speeder bikes through jungle terrain, sneaking up on enemy positions to make sudden strikes. The bikes are fast and can turn amazingly quickly, allowing them to dodge laser fire and keep one step ahead of the enemy.

Clone Specialist

Identified by their red armor coloring, clone shock troopers are an elite corps of soldiers. They are trained in guerrilla tactics and are used in tricky battlefield situations where deadly cunning and keen instincts are the only recipe for success.

Aliens and Droids

The Clone Wars affect all the galaxy's inhabitants, from powerful Wookiees to peaceful Utapauns—even lowly droids. Everyone is forced to take sides, either Separatist or Republic.

Wookiee Warrior
Tarfful helps his fellow Wookiees to defend their planet from invading droid armies. He carries a heavy, powerful Wookiee blaster.

Eye In The Sky
On the occupied planet Utapau, General Grievous dispatches a small seeker droid to locate Obi-Wan after he falls into the waters of a deep sinkhole.

Hostage of War
Tion Medon lives on the captured planet Utapau, where the Separatists have a secret base. He helps Obi-Wan Kenobi when the Jedi arrives to pursue General Grievous.

Furry Support
Chewbacca is a brave Wookiee who helps Yoda when the Jedi Master arrives to protect the Wookiee planet Kashyyyk. He will also help Yoda leave the planet when the Jedi is in danger.

Strong-armed Support
If the Separatists destroy a Republic gunship or military base, the clone commanders send in teams of pincer droids to rescue any scraps of machinery that can be reused.

Droids Everywhere
Astromech droids are helping in the war effort by acting as capable copilots for the Jedi Knights in their starfighters. Many of them are destroyed in battle.

Silent Medics
These alien doctors communicate without speech and run a medical center on an asteroid called Polis Massa. They assist at the birth of Padmé Amidala's children.

Slimy Senators
Many greedy Senators support the Separatist troublemakers. But they will receive no help from Palpatine after he proclaims himself Emperor, with total power over the galaxy.

HEROES AND VILLAINS

Yoda

Swamp Speeder

General
Grievous

Seeker
Droid

Obi-Wan Kenobi

Anakin's
Starfighter

Clone Pilot

Naboo
Blaster

General
Grievous

Count
Dooku

Droid Gunship

Tion Medon

Grievous's
Blaster

mé
ala

Darth
Vader

Astromech
Droid

HEROES AND VILLAINS

Anakin

Tri-Fighter

Ki-Adi-Mundi

AT-RT

Nute
Gunray

C-3PO and
R2-D2

Star
Destroyer

Chewbacca

Clone
Trooper

Separatist
Starship

Bail Organa

Dooku and Anakin in Battle

Wat
Tambor

Utapau Blaster

Grievous's
Fighter

HEROES AND VILLAINS

Swamp Speeder

Yoda

General
Grievous

Seeker
Droid

Obi-Wan Kenobi

Anakin's
Starfighter

Clone Pilot

Naboo
Blaster

General
Grievous

Count
Dooku

Droid Gunship

Tion Medon

Grievous's
Blaster

Padmé
Amidala

Darth
Vader

Astromech
Droid

HEROES AND VILLAINS

Anakin

Tri-Fighter

Ki-Adi-Mundi

AT-RT

Nute
Gunray

C-3PO and
R2-D2

Star
Destroyer

Chewbacca

Clone
Trooper

Separatist
Starship

Wat
Tambor

Bail Organa

Dooku and Anakin in Battle

Utapau Blaster

Grievous's
Fighter

Speeder Bike

Pilot Anakin

Mace Windu

Buzz Droid

Plo Koon's Starfighter

Darth Sidious

Pincer Droid

Magnaguard

Clone Trooper

Commander Bly

Tank Droid

Clone Trooper

Clone Trooper

Agen Kolar

Clone Trooper

HEROES AND VILLAINS

Speeder Bike

Pilot Anakin

Mace Windu

Buzz Droid

Plo Koon's Starfighter

Darth Sidious

Pincer Droid

Magnaguard

Clone Trooper

Commander Bly

Tank Droid

Clone Trooper

Clone Trooper

Agen Kolar

Clone Trooper

HEROES AND VILLAINS

ARC-170

Tarfful

Missile

Anakin Skywalker

Polis Massan

Blaster

Space Battle

V-wing

Passel
Argente

Crab Droid

Kit Fisto

Senator

Clone
Trooper

Shaak Ti

Obi-Wan's Starfighter

Vulture Droid

HEROES AND VILLAINS

ARC-170

Tarfful

Missile

Anakin Skywalker

Polis Massan

Space Battle

Blaster

V-wing

Crab Droid

Passel
Argente

Kit Fisto

Senator

Clone
Trooper

Shaak Ti

-Wan's Starfighter

Vulture Droid

CLASSIC TRILOGY

The Empire

From the moment the Emperor took control of the Old Republic, renaming it the Galactic Empire, the galaxy has been threatened by tyranny and evil. The Emperor ruthlessly uses the dark side of the Force to control his subjects. Protected by a vast army of lethal machines and sinister generals, he will stop at nothing to expand the realms of Imperial power.

Loyal Guard
Fanatically loyal, the mysterious Imperial Royal Guards protect the Emperor. They are highly trained in deadly arts and use vibro-active force pikes to inflict lethal wounds.

Dark Knight
Prowling the corridors of the Imperial Navy, Darth Vader is a much-feared military commander. He was once a pupil of the Jedi Obi-Wan Kenobi, but now works for the Emperor. Vader's knowledge of the dark side of the Force makes him extremely dangerous.

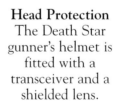

White Fighter
Highly disciplined and loyal to the Emperor, the stormtroopers are shielded by white space armor. They are the most trusted and effective troops in the Imperial military.

Lethal Weapon
Darth Vader's lightsaber has a blade of pure energy that can cut through nearly any object.

Head Protection
The Death Star gunner's helmet is fitted with a transceiver and a shielded lens.

Close Shot
The standard blaster is issued to every scout trooper. This weapon is ideal for short-range targets.

Double Bomber
The Empire's main bomber is the TIE assault bomber. It is exceptionally successful on ground-bombing missions.

Evil Dictator
Drawing his powers from the dark side of the Force, the terrible Emperor rules the military forces of the Imperial Navy. His simple clothing and hood conceal his twisted features.

Accurate Shot
This rugged laser rifle has incredible consistency and accuracy.

Controlled Power
The lethal TIE Interceptor has dagger-shaped solar panels. It also has special ion drives that give the pilot extra control.

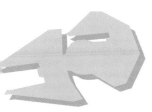

Torturer
The pitiless interrogator droid surgically exploits every weakness it finds in the enemy.

Lone Trooper
Scout troopers are trained to endure long periods without support. They are only armored on the upper body and head.

Terrorizer
These fearsome wedge-shaped warships are called Star Destroyers. They carry devastating firepower throughout the galaxy to terrorize any opposition.

Tough Walker
The gigantic All Terrain Armored Transport (AT-AT) walkers are invulnerable to most blaster bolts and cannons.

Agile Fighter
The small TIE fighter is built for high-speed maneuvres.

Fast Walker
The All Terrain Scout Transport (AT-ST) is known as the scout walker. Fast and agile, it can travel over rough terrain in search of hidden enemy groups.

Ultimate Weapon
Invulnerable to large-scale assault, the Death Star contains a hypermatter reactor that can generate enough power to destroy an entire planet.

Stormtrooper Blaster
Compact and rugged, the E-11 BlasTech Standard Imperial sidearm combines excellent range with lethal firepower.

Probe Droid
Intelligent and eerie, the probe droid is equipped with myriad sensors and investigative instinct.

Galactic Life

The galaxy is teeming with mysterious creatures and beings. Many of these are outlaws, who try to survive beyond the Empire's grasp. Jawas trade in scavenged junk and droid parts; Jabba the Hutt masterminds a criminal empire all his own; and even musicians sometimes gamble their way out of debt. And then there are the bounty hunters, who thrive by their murderous and violent deeds.

Explosive device
Carried at the back of the belt, the thermal detonator contains powerful explosives.

Vile Crime Lord
Astute and ruthless, Jabba the Hutt is at the center of a large criminal empire. He eats nine meals a day and enjoys using his power and wealth to control weaker species.

Notorious Hunter
Cool and calculating, the mysterious Boba Fett is the best bounty hunter in the galaxy. He has his own code of honor and only takes on missions that meet his harsh sense of justice.

Swindler's Tool
Used by the swindling Jawas, ionization blasters feature built-in ion regulators and a blast nozzle.

Military Droid
The RA-7 Protocol Droid is a military model designed to work closely with the latest E-wing fighter.

Pleasure Craft
Jabba the Hutt's sail barge, Khetanna, is used to transport the crimelord wherever he wishes to go.

Musical Minds
Naturally musical and intelligent, the band called the Modal Nodes is the most often heard in the Mos Eisley Cantina. Their lead player, Figrin D'an, is an experienced gambler who manages to keep the band out of trouble.

Stalking Ship
Boba Fett's deceptive starship, *Slave I*, is fitted with a stolen secret sensor-masking device, enabling it to disappear from most scanning systems.

Sand Patrol
Rusted and scoured by countless sandstorms, the Jawa sandcrawler searches the wastelands of Tatooine for lost droids and salvagable junk.

Criminal Minds
Bossk is a reptilian Trandoshan and a tough bounty hunter. 4-LOM was once a sophisticated protocol droid, but has degraded to become a criminal.

Fearsome Carnivore
Kept in a pit by Jabba the Hutt, the fearsome rancor is five metres (16 feet) tall and has an armored skin.

Sand Creature
Prowling through the dunes and wastes of Tatooine, Tusken Raiders are masters of the desert. Savage and violent, they can survive where no one else can.

Tough Guard
Brutish, stubborn and often violent, the Gamorrean guards protect Jabba's palace. They prefer to use hand-to-hand combat weapons instead of blasters.

Scavengers
Dressed in dark robes, the notoriously tricky Jawas patrol the dunes looking for junk to repair and trade.

Killer Instincts
Trained as an Imperial assassin, Dengar had brain surgery that turned him into a merciless killer. The IG-88 assassin droid is no less vile: it escaped from the laboratories and now stalks the galaxy, obsessed with killing.

Hungry Player
The crazy keyboard player, Max Rebo, is a blue Ortolan. He is so obsessed with food that he asked Jabba to pay him in free meals.

Fearsome Criminal
As Jabba's chief lieutenant, the conniving Bib Fortuna uses underhanded methods to gain control. Despite his obsequious manner, he is always plotting a way to kill his boss.

The Rebellion

Fighting to rid the galaxy of Imperial tyranny, the Rebel Alliance relies on the light side of the Force. The Rebels are a diverse group made up of royalty, exiled aliens, droids, ex-smugglers, and Jedi Knights. Together they try to overcome the evil powers of darkness.

Steady Fire
Designed by Admiral Ackbar, the B-wing fighter has an unusual gyrostabilization system that keeps the cockpit steady while the pilot fires at the enemy.

Communication
Comlinks enable individual soldiers to communicate with other Rebels while on patrol or performing other military duties.

Young Hero
Determined and innovative, the heroic Luke Skywalker transformed himself from farmboy to wing commander for the Alliance. His natural ability to respond to the Force means he is a born leader, with the qualities to become a noble Jedi Knight.

Stern Beauty
Strong-willed, disciplined and beautiful, Princess Leia is the youngest-ever Galactic Senator and has her own consular ship, *Tantive IV*. She uses her powerful position to help the Rebel Alliance.

Action Man
Confident, rugged and reckless, Han Solo has worked his way up from poor beginnings to become captain of the *Falcon*. His gunfighting skills make him a match for any adversary.

Hard Target
The Incom T-47 airspeeder, nicknamed snowspeeder, is used for low atmospheric duty. It can reach more than 1,000 km (620 miles) per hour, and although it has no shield, its compact size makes it hard to hit.

Hoth Essentials
On the ice planet Hoth, Rebels must carry all their equipment in a special backpack.

Energy Blaster
The DH-17 Rebel blaster uses high energy blaster gases to shoot bolts of light energy.

Ocean Friend
Commander of the Rebel fleet, the cautious Admiral Ackbar comes from the ocean world of Mon Calamari. His ships, the giant Mon Cal star cruisers, are the largest in the Rebel fleet.

Mysterious Hermit
Once a great warrior of the Old Republic, the mysterious Ben Kenobi is a Jedi Knight who lives in the Jundland Wastes. His vast powers and knowledge of the Force make him a threat to the Empire.

Escape Route
This simple escape pod can propel C-3PO and R2-D2 away from danger with its basic rocket engine.

Speed Machine
Ideal for hit-and-run missions, the lightweight A-wing fighter was designed to outrun any Imperial ship.

Head Gear
The insulated Rebel helmet is marked with the Alliance symbol.

Etiquette Master
As a protocol droid fluent in more than six million forms of communication, C-3PO is programmed to ensure that everything runs smoothly. Although he is often overwhelmed by the turbulent times, he always remains faithful to his masters.

Mighty Wookiee
Rescued from slavery by Han Solo, the mighty Wookiee Chewbacca uses his mechanical skills to keep Solo's spaceship flying. He is fiercely loyal and a perfect fighting partner for Han Solo.

Loyal Servant
The quirky R2-D2 was designed as a sophisticated computer repair and information retrieval droid. He is always prepared to risk destruction to help his masters.

Rebel Craft

To survive the terrifying power of the Empire, the Rebel Alliance needs a vast range of fighter ships, special equipment, and, perhaps most importantly, expert advice.

Rogue Leader
The stylish Lando Calrissian, once a roguish smuggler captain, is the flamboyant leader of Cloud City. He has a head for business and skilful judgment in battle.

Premier Fighter
One of the most impressive fighters in the Rebel force, the T-65 X-wing is extremely durable. Designed to carry heavy weapons, it is also remarkably maneuverable.

Furry Friends
Small and furry, the resourceful Ewoks live in the forests of the emerald moon, Endor.

Computer Pack
The Rebel sensor pack is fitted with a range cycle computer and a stentronic wave monitor.

High Maintenance
Despite its battered and ageing appearance, Han Solo's *Millennium Falcon* is one of the fastest ships in the galaxy.

Durable Fighter
Before the introduction of the X-wing starfighter, the Y-wing was the main fighter for the Alliance. Built to last, it is still widely used as a combination fighter and light bomber.

Wise Teacher
At almost 900 years old, Jedi Master Yoda is very powerful with the Force. It is his duty to try and instill in Luke a faith, peace, and harmony that will protect him from the evil powers of the dark side.

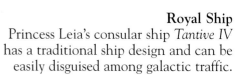

Royal Ship
Princess Leia's consular ship *Tantive IV* has a traditional ship design and can be easily disguised among galactic traffic.

CHARACTERS AND CREATURES

Boba Fett

Obi-Wan Kenobi

Tusken
Raider

Luke Skywalker

Princess
Leia

Han
Solo

Darth
Vader

Bib
Fortuna

Emperor Palpatine

Admiral Ackbar

Jabba the Hutt

Boba Fett

Obi-Wan Kenobi

Tusken
Raider

Luke Skywalker

Princess
Leia

Han
Solo

Darth
Vader

Bib
Fortuna

Emperor Palpatine

Admiral Ackbar

Jabba the Hutt

SPACECRAFT, VEHICLES, DROIDS, AND EQUIPMENT

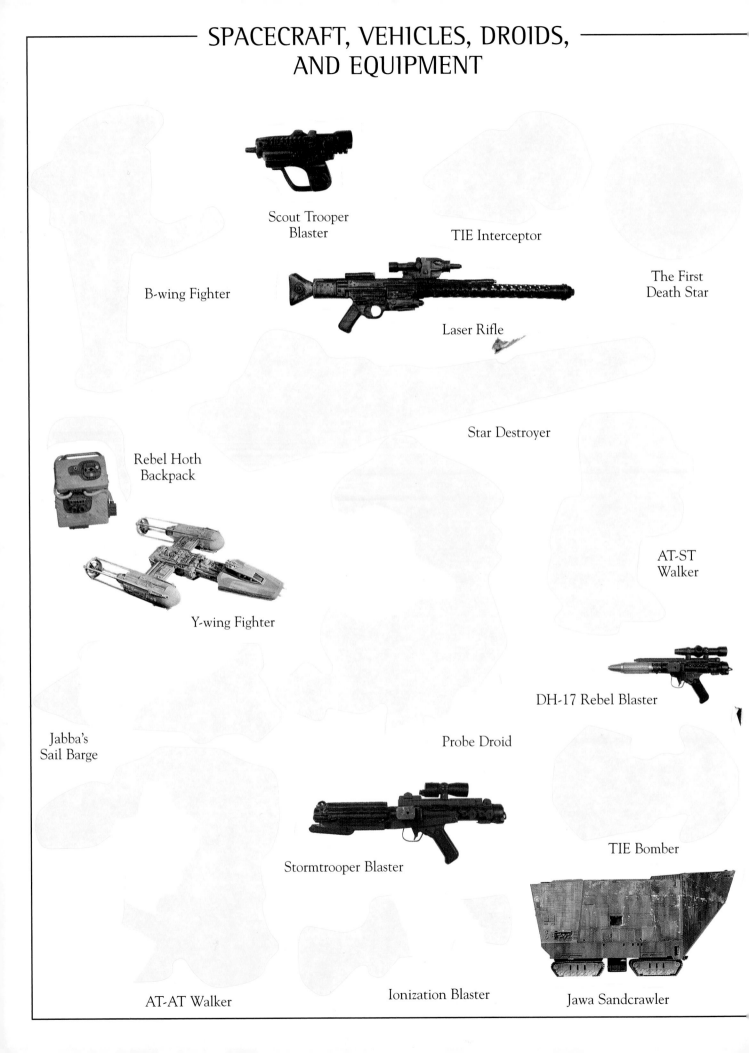

Scout Trooper
Blaster

TIE Interceptor

B-wing Fighter

The First
Death Star

Laser Rifle

Star Destroyer

Rebel Hoth
Backpack

AT-ST
Walker

Y-wing Fighter

DH-17 Rebel Blaster

Jabba's
Sail Barge

Probe Droid

TIE Bomber

Stormtrooper Blaster

AT-AT Walker

Ionization Blaster

Jawa Sandcrawler

SPACECRAFT, VEHICLES, DROIDS, AND EQUIPMENT

Darth Vader's
Lightsaber

Rebel Helmet

T-65 X-wing

R2-D2

A-wing
Fighter

Slave I

Interrogator
Droid

Comlink

C-3PO

Death Star
Gunner's
Helmet

Millennium Falcon

TIE Fighter

Boushh's Thermal
Detonator

Rebel Sensor Pack

C-3PO and
R2-D2's
Escape Pod

RA-7
Protocol
Droid

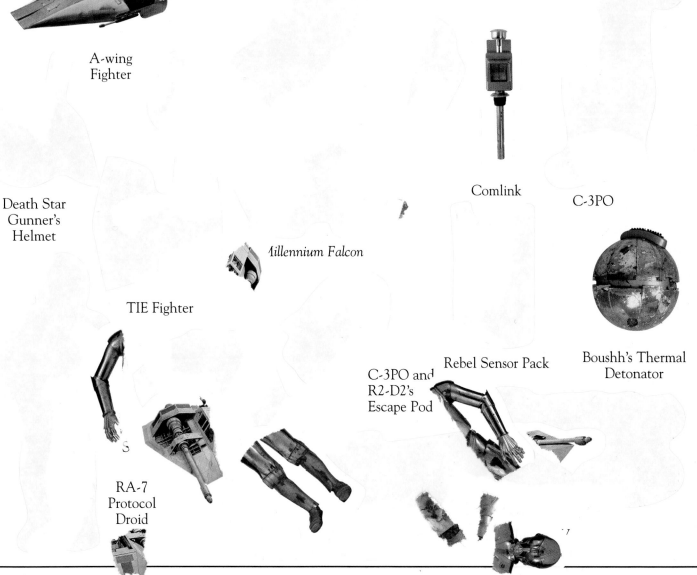

SPACECRAFT, VEHICLES, DROIDS, AND EQUIPMENT

T-65 X-wing

Darth Vader's Lightsaber

Rebel Helmet

R2-D2

Slave I

Interrogator Droid

A-wing Fighter

Comlink

C-3PO

Death Star Gunner's Helmet

Millennium Falcon

TIE Fighter

Rebel Sensor Pack

Boushh's Thermal Detonator

C-3PO and R2-D2's Escape Pod

Snowspeeder

RA-7 Protocol Droid

Tantive IV

Chewbacca

Gamorrean
Guard

Ewok

Dengar and IG-88

Imperial
Royal
Guard

Stormtrooper

Bossk and 4-LOM

Rancor

Yoda

Lando
Calrissian

Scout Trooper

Jawa

Max Rebo

Modal Nodes

CHARACTERS AND CREATURES

Chewbacca

Gamorrean
Guard

Ewok

Dengar and IG-88

Imperial
Royal
Guard

Stormtrooper

Bossk and 4-LOM

Lando
Calrissian

Yoda

Rancor

Scout Trooper

Max Rebo

Jawa

Modal Nodes